P9-BYV-602

PIES

Mini Pies

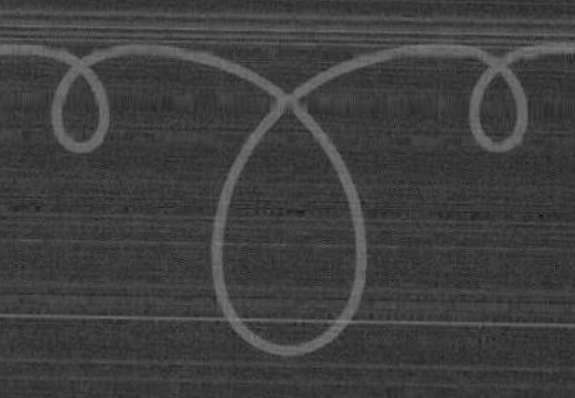

Abigail Johnson Dodge

photographs
Lauren Burke

weldonowen

Contents

all about mini pies

There's nothing more irresistible than a homemade pie and mini pies are no exception. Just about anything sweet or savory can be tucked inside these single-serving pies: summer fruits, fresh vegetables, or even tender steak. Mini pies are perfect in every way, whether served à la mode for dessert or alongside a tangy salad for lunch.

Pies are popular baked goods in kitchens around the world. We make them for parties and bake sales, when we're craving a special treat on a lazy Sunday, or when we've found ourselves with a bumper crop of summer fruits or winter squashes. Making a pie can be time consuming, and some busy cooks will purchase them instead of making them from scratch. The introduction of the electric pie maker changes everything.

Mini pies are just as robust as their larger counterparts, and they're more convenient to make and share with a hungry audience. These little pies require little more than a basic dough—purchased at the store or homemade—as well as a few minutes to put together a filling and another moment to assemble them in an electric pie maker.

Making these pies is fast and breezy work, and this book walks you through it all step by step. Beginning with an information-packed section that covers the equipment you'll need, the types of doughs and fillings that can be used, and tips for success, you'll be armed with everything you need to know to make delicious mini pies in minutes. Next, you'll find 40 delicious recipes for pies that take about 10 minutes to bake to perfection in an electric pie maker. Recipes include savory options such as breakfast quiches, Cornish pasties filled with peas and carrots, and an onion-tartlike variation. Among the book's classic dessert pies are plenty of versatile recipes that showcase the best of summer berries, crunchy pecans, and tender figs. The book ends with detailed instructions on how to cut and shape the dough and make a lattice top, as well as basic recipes for glazes and freshly whipped cream to top the pies. There is also an all-purpose recipe for homemade pie dough.

More than just a delicious, individual-sized dessert, mini pies also make a great light meal or snack. Pack a picnic basket full of quiches or other savory pies alongside seasonal fruit pies for your next outing. Or, create a whole spread of traditional favorites for your next holiday party—just don't count on any leftovers!

equipment

Making mini pies requires less time and no more equipment than large pies. Aside from an electric pie maker, and its accompanying tools, all you will need are a few simple items for preparing these treats.

electric pie maker Available in kitchenware stores and online retailers, electric pie makers are entirely modern. They have four round wells with 4-inch (10 cm) diameters. Once the lid is closed, the maker molds and seals four perfectly crimped pies and then cooks them to golden perfection. When the pies are done, the nonstick coating on the surface allows for easy removal.

After a quick initial seasoning with a little vegetable oil rubbed into the cooking plates (follow the manufacturer's instructions), the machine is ready to use with any of the recipes in this book.

pastry cutter Included with the electric pie maker, the pastry cutter takes the guesswork out of creating the right size crusts for mini pies. It features two sides that cut the dough into two sizes: small and large. Use the large side for cutting out the bottom crust and small side for cutting out the top (if using). For more information on cutting the dough, see page 87.

pastry press The electric pie maker includes a customized pastry press which is needed to mold the pie dough into a crust once it is placed into the mini pie maker. For more information on molding, see page 87.

measuring utensils Metal measuring cups and spoons are best for measuring dry ingredients, as metal is more durable than plastic. For measuring liquids, glass pitchers, in 1-cup (8–fl oz/250-ml) or 2-cup (16–fl oz/500-ml) sizes are a good choice.

mixing bowls Choose a good-quality nesting set of stainless-steel bowls, which are durable and can be heated. Other alternative materials include ceramic and glass bowls. Avoid aluminum bowls, which react to acidic foods, and plastic bowls, which absorb odors and fats.

whisks & spatulas A metal wire whisk is perfect for whipping up fillings and cream. Choose one with a metal handle and sturdy loops of wire. Choose a few well-made spatulas. You'll need a flat metal spatula for lifting and transferring dough and a small offset spatula for removing the finished mini pies from the pie maker.

frying pan Since the baking time for mini pies is so short, many fillings need to be precooked on the stovetop in a frying pan. It's a good idea to have on hand a small 9- to 10-inch (23- to 25-cm) and a larger 12- to 14-inch (30- to 35-cm) frying pan.

fork A metal dinner fork is needed to aid in removing the baked pie from the electric pie maker. Choose one made of sturdy metal.

the parts of the pie

Pies are made up of two key players: the crust and the filling. Both add texture and flavor and are what set this delectable pastry apart from other baked goods.

the crust

Flaky and buttery, the crust is the structural component of the pie. In the electric pie maker, sturdy pie dough works best as the bottom crust. For a top crust, light and flaky puff pastry and filo dough work best.

pie dough One 9- to 9½-inch (23- to 24-cm) round of pie dough yields four mini pie bases or tops. For most recipes, you'll need just one round for a bottom crust. Purchased pie dough will work for every recipe in this book, but if you would like to make your own, see page 91.

puff pastry dough Puff pastry is used as the top crust for many pies in this book. Its thin flaky layers are delicious and work well in the electric pie maker. One 8-by-10-inch (20-by-25-cm) sheet of dough yields four tops and can be purchased in most markets. Be sure to keep it frozen until use, thaw the dough in the refrigerator just before using.

filo dough Sheets of filo dough, usually 12 by 18 inches (30 by 45 cm) in size, can be used for a top crust and are another good option for the electric pie maker. Purchase sheets in the refrigerated section of the market.

tips & tricks

Here are a few useful tips and reminders to help you make prize-worthy mini pies every time.

- Preheat the pie maker twice before making your first batch of pies. This will ensure even cooking and well-browned crusts.
- After the pie maker has preheated, the surface will be extremely hot. Be extra careful when working with and near the maker to avoid burns.
- To ensure even cooking and heat distribution in the pie maker, bake four pies at a time.
- Keep in mind that no more than ⅓ cup (3 fl oz/80 ml) of filling should be used for each mini pie.
- The pie maker has a nonstick surface, so opt for utensils that won't scratch the finish when removing pies.
- If you're feeding a crowd, recipes can easily be doubled or tripled to make 8 or 12 pies.
- Baked pies can be warmed in the preheated electric pie maker for 3–5 minutes or in a preheated 425°F (220°C) oven for 10 minutes.

For more tips & tricks for working with dough, see page 88.

the filling

In the best pie fillings, the main ingredients are showcased simply and with little fuss. In most cases you'll need to precook everything before it goes into the electric pie maker. Avoid any sauces, gravies, or thin custards as they can overflow and turn a crust soggy. Drier, firmer fillings work best.

cheeses Soft cheeses or those that melt easily—such as feta, mozzarella, Swiss, manchego, and Gruyère—are delicious in mini pies. You'll only need a small amount to add alongside vegetables, for a pie filling or combine cheese with eggs to make a quiche. For the best flavor, buy cheeses from a local cheese shop or market that sells their stock quickly.

chocolate Mixed with other ingredients such as graham crackers and nuts or cream cheese (for a cheesecake-like pie), chocolate works well inside a mini pie crust and it won't turn the crust wet and soggy. Choose high-quality bittersweet and milk varieties.

eggs Eggs help bind fillings, but as a star ingredient inside breakfast pies or quiches, they make a quick and easy meal that can be enjoyed hot or at room temperature. When purchasing, choose fresh large Grade A eggs.

fruits Pies are a wonderful way to celebrate stone fruit, berries, figs, apples, citrus, and tropical fruits picked at the peak of their season. Inside a pie crust, the naturally juicy fruits cook in their own syrup, intensifying their flavor. To punch up any fruit that lacks acidity, add a few drops of fresh lemon juice. Seek out the highest quality fruit you can find, buying it in its peak season.

meats & seafood Salmon, chicken, ham, steak, and ground meats take a mini pie from a snack to a meal. They are the perfect pairing with vegetables, herbs, and flaky pastry. You'll need to cook the meats ahead of time before placing in the pie maker—an easy task, especially if you use leftovers. For the best flavor, purchase meats and seafood from a local source with high turnover.

nuts Nuts can be sliced, toasted, and mixed with sugar before being added to a pie. Pecans are a natural pie filling, and almonds, especially finely ground and mixed with eggs, transform humble pie into a decadent treat. To ensure freshness, store nuts in the freezer.

purées Root vegetables, such as sweet potatoes and pumpkins, and fruits such as apples and pears make great pies when roasted and puréed into a velvety smooth filling. Make your own or seek out high-quality canned or bottled purées.

vegetables Greens, onions, mushrooms, peas, carrots, potatoes, and turnips add nutritional substance and satisfaction to mini pies. Most require a little cooking on the stovetop before they're added to the electric pie maker. Buy fresh, seasonal vegetables whenever possible.

Sweet Pies

These speedy mini pies bake up in a fraction of the time it takes to make a full-size pie. Make sure to use sweet, ripe peaches. They will smell fragrant and give slightly near the stem when gently pressed.

summer peach pies

- 2 teaspoons cornstarch
- 2 teaspoons fresh lemon juice
- 2 ripe peaches (about 5 oz/155 g each), halved, pitted, and cut into ½-inch (12-mm) pieces
- 3 tablespoons firmly packed golden brown sugar
- Pinch of salt
- ¼ teaspoon pure vanilla extract
- 1 pie dough round for a 9- to 9½-inch (23- to 24-cm) pie (page 10)
- 1 frozen all-butter prepared puff pastry sheet (about 4 oz/125 g), thawed (page 10)
- Vanilla ice cream for serving (optional)

makes 4 pies

To make the filling, stir together the cornstarch and lemon juice in a small bowl until the cornstarch dissolves. Set aside. In a frying pan over medium-low heat, cook the peaches, brown sugar, and salt, stirring until the sugar has dissolved, about 2 minutes. Stir the cornstarch mixture and pour into the pan. Bring to a boil, continuing to stir. Boil until the peaches are tender when pierced with a fork, about 1 minute. Remove from the heat. Add the vanilla. Stir gently to coat the peaches with the liquid. Set aside.

Following the manufacturer's instructions, preheat the electric pie maker until ready to use. Meanwhile, using the accompanying pastry cutter, cut the pie dough into 4 large rounds and cut the puff pastry into 4 small rounds. (For more information on cutting the dough, see page 87.)

Working quickly, place each large pie dough round into the pie maker. Using the accompanying pastry press, mold the dough into the wells to form the bottom crusts. (For more information on molding, see page 87.) Divide the filling among the crusts and spread evenly. Place a small puff pastry round over each filled crust.

Following the manufacturer's instructions, bake the pies until the crusts are well browned, about 10 minutes. Using a fork, lift one edge of a pie just enough to slide a small offset spatula under the bottom and transfer to a wire rack to cool slightly. Repeat with the remaining pies. Serve warm with vanilla ice cream, if using.

This classic fresh fruit filling—a perfect balance between sweet and tart—re-imagines a favorite dessert as individual-size pies. It is the perfect treat to celebrate the beginning of summer.

strawberry-rhubarb pies

7–9 strawberries (about 7 oz/220 g total), rinsed and patted dry

2 oz (60 g) rhubarb, rinsed and dried

1 tablespoon unsalted butter

4 tablespoons granulated sugar

1 tablespoon all-purpose flour

½ teaspoon finely grated orange zest

Pinch of salt

1 pie dough round for a 9- to 9½-inch (23- to 24-cm) pie (page 10)

2 frozen all-butter prepared puff pastry sheets (about 4 oz/125 g each), thawed (page 10)

Vanilla ice cream for serving (optional)

makes 4 pies

To make the filling, stem and coarsely chop the strawberries (you should have about 1½ cups/6 oz/180 g). Set aside. Cut the rhubarb into ½-inch (12-mm) pieces (about ½ cup/2½ oz/75 g). Melt the butter in a small frying pan over low heat. Add the rhubarb and cook, stirring, until very tender, 7–9 minutes. Remove from the heat. Add the strawberries, sugar, flour, orange zest, and salt. Stir until well blended. Set aside to cool.

Following the manufacturer's instructions, preheat the electric pie maker until ready to use. Meanwhile, using the accompanying pastry cutter, cut the pie dough into 4 large rounds (see page 87). Following the instructions on page 88, cut and shape the puff pastry into 4 lattice tops.

Working quickly, place each large pie dough round into the pie maker. Using the accompanying pastry press, mold the dough into the wells to form the bottom crusts. (For more information on molding, see page 87.) Divide the filling among the crusts and spread evenly. Place a lattice round over each filled crust.

Following the manufacturer's instructions, bake the pies until the crusts are well browned, about 10 minutes. Using a fork, carefully lift one edge of a pie just enough to slide a small offset spatula under the bottom and transfer to a wire rack to cool slightly or completely. Repeat with the remaining pies. Serve warm or at room temperature with vanilla ice cream, if using.

Strawberry picking is a summertime ritual for many families. Continue the fun indoors by baking the harvest into these tiny pies with your kids' help. To double the flavor, serve them warm with fresh strawberry ice cream.

fresh strawberry pies

1 pie dough round for a 9- to 9½-inch (23- to 24-cm) pie (page 10)

1 frozen all-butter prepared puff pastry sheet (about 4 oz/125 g), thawed (page 10)

10–12 strawberries, (about 8 oz/250 g total), rinsed and patted dry

2 teaspoons fresh lemon juice

3 tablespoons granulated sugar

2 teaspoons all-purpose flour

½ teaspoon finely grated lemon zest

Pinch of salt

Strawberry ice cream for serving (optional)

makes 4 pies

Following the manufacturer's instructions, preheat the electric pie maker until ready to use. Meanwhile, using the accompanying pastry cutter, cut the pie dough into 4 large rounds and cut the puff pastry into 4 small rounds. (For more information on cutting the dough, see page 87.)

To make the filling, stem and coarsely chop the strawberries. In a bowl, combine the strawberries, lemon juice, sugar, flour, lemon zest, and salt. Stir gently to coat evenly.

Working quickly, place each large pie dough round into the pie maker. Using the accompanying pastry press, mold the dough into the wells to form the bottom crusts. (For more information on molding, see page 87.) Divide the filling among the crusts and spread evenly. Place a small puff pastry round over each filled crust.

Following the manufacturer's instructions, bake the pies until the crusts are well browned, about 10 minutes. Using a fork, carefully lift one edge of a pie just enough to slide a small offset spatula under the bottom and transfer to a wire rack to cool slightly or completely. Repeat with the remaining pies. Serve warm or at room temperature with strawberry ice cream, if using.

Here's another great recipe to try after a day of berry picking. Crystallized ginger lends a peppery nuance to the filling. Choose ginger pieces that are thick and moist-looking for the best flavor and texture.

blackberry-ginger pies

- 1 pie dough round for a 9- to 9½-inch (23- to 24-cm) pie (page 10)
- 1 frozen all-butter prepared puff pastry sheet (about 4 oz/125 g), thawed (page 10)
- ¾ pint (9 oz/280 g) blackberries, rinsed and patted dry
- ⅓ cup (3 oz/90 g) granulated sugar
- 5 teaspoons all-purpose flour
- 1 tablespoon finely chopped crystallized ginger
- 1½ teaspoons fresh lemon juice
- Pinch of salt
- Vanilla ice cream for serving (optional)

makes 4 pies

Following the manufacturer's instructions, preheat the electric pie maker until ready to use. Meanwhile, using the accompanying pastry cutter, cut the pie dough into 4 large rounds and cut the puff pastry into 4 small rounds. (For more information on cutting the dough, see page 87.)

To make the filling, combine the blackberries, sugar, flour, ginger, lemon juice, and salt in a bowl. Stir the mixture until the berries are lightly crushed and evenly coated.

Working quickly, place each large pie dough round into the pie maker. Using the accompanying pastry press, mold the dough into the wells to form the bottom crusts. (For more information on molding, see page 87.) Divide the filling among the crusts and spread evenly. Place a small puff pastry round over each filled crust.

Following the manufacturer's instructions, bake the pies until the crusts are well browned, about 10 minutes. Using a fork, carefully lift one edge of a pie just enough to slide a small offset spatula under the bottom and transfer to a wire rack to cool slightly or completely. Repeat with the remaining pies. Serve warm or at room temperature with vanilla ice cream, if using.

This version of the iconic childhood treat can be made all year long—no campfire necessary. These pies can be made ahead of time and reheated in the pie maker for a few minutes—just long enough to melt the chocolate.

s'more pies

1 pie dough round for a 9- to 9½-inch (23- to 24-cm) pie (page 10)

2 cinnamon or plain graham crackers

3 bars (1.55 oz/43 g each) milk chocolate

¼ cup (1 oz/30 g) chopped pecans (optional)

4 standard-size marshmallows

makes 4 pies

Following the manufacturer's instructions, preheat the electric pie maker until ready to use. Meanwhile, using the accompanying pastry cutter, cut the pie dough into 4 large rounds. (For more information on cutting the dough, see page 87.)

Break the graham crackers into small pieces no bigger than ½ inch (12 mm). Break the chocolate bars into small rectangles. Divide the graham crackers, chocolate, and pecans, if using, into 4 equal piles.

Working quickly, place each pie dough round into the pie maker. Using the accompanying pastry press, mold the dough into the wells to form the bottom crusts. (For more information on molding, see page 87.) Distribute the graham crackers equally among the crusts. Put the chocolate pieces on top of the crackers. Divide the pecans, if using, evenly among the crusts.

Following the manufacturer's instructions, bake the pies until the crusts are well browned, about 10 minutes. Using a fork, carefully lift one edge of a pie just enough to slide a small offset spatula under the bottom and transfer to a wire rack. Repeat with the remaining pies. Place a marshmallow on top of each pie and serve right away. (If you prefer melted marshmallows, like those shown in the photo, place the marshmallow-topped baked pies under a broiler for 3–5 minutes.)

Summer offers a bounty of fresh berries to use for baking. Select sweet, plump berries with no signs of bruising or mold. You can use any mixture of berries measuring no more than 1⅓ cups (6½ oz/195 g).

mixed berry pies

1 pie dough round for a 9- to 9½-inch (23- to 24-cm) pie (page 10)

1 frozen all-butter prepared puff pastry sheet (about 4 oz/125 g), thawed (page 10)

3 fresh strawberries, (about 3 oz/90 g total), rinsed and patted dry

½ cup (2 oz/60 g) raspberries, rinsed and patted dry

½ cup (2 oz/60 g) blueberries, rinsed and patted dry

3 tablespoons firmly packed golden brown sugar

4 teaspoons cornstarch

1 teaspoon fresh lemon juice

½ teaspoon finely grated orange zest

Pinch of salt

Whipped Cream (page 90) for serving (optional)

makes 4 pies

Following the manufacturer's instructions, preheat the electric pie maker until ready to use. Meanwhile, using the accompanying pastry cutter, cut the pie dough into 4 large rounds and cut the puff pastry into 4 small rounds. (For more information on cutting the dough, see page 87.)

To make the filling, stem and coarsely chop the strawberries. In a bowl, combine the strawberries, raspberries, blueberries, brown sugar, cornstarch, lemon juice, orange zest, and salt. Stir gently to coat. You should have about 1⅓ cups (6½ oz/195 g) of filling.

Working quickly, place each large pie dough round into the pie maker. Using the accompanying pastry press, mold the dough into the wells to form the bottom crusts. (For more information on molding, see page 87.) Divide the filling among the crusts and spread evenly. Place a small puff pastry round over each filled crust.

Following the manufacturer's instructions, bake the pies until the crusts are well browned, about 10 minutes. Using a fork, carefully lift one edge of a pie just enough to slide a small offset spatula under the bottom and transfer to a wire rack to cool slightly or completely. Repeat with the remaining pies. Serve warm or at room temperature with a dollop of whipped cream, if using.

Frangipane is made with finely ground nuts—in this case, almonds—that are thickened with eggs to form a custardlike base. For the strongest almond flavor, toast the nuts before and add the optional almond extract.

almond frangipane pies

- 1 pie dough round for a 9- to 9½-inch (23- to 24-cm) pie (page 10)
- 1 cup (4 oz/120 g) plus 2 tablespoons sliced almonds, toasted
- ½ cup (4 oz/125 g) granulated sugar
- 5 tablespoons (2½ oz/75 g) unsalted butter, at room temperature
- 1 large egg, plus 1 yolk from large egg
- 1 teaspoon pure vanilla extract
- ¼ teaspoon pure almond extract (optional)
- Raspberries or ripe figs for serving (optional)
- Confectioners' sugar for dusting (optional)

makes 4 pies

Following the manufacturer's instructions, preheat the electric pie maker until ready to use. Meanwhile, using the accompanying pastry cutter, cut the pie dough into 4 large rounds. (For more information on cutting the dough, see page 87.)

To make the filling, in a food processor, combine 1 cup of the toasted almonds and the sugar. Process until the mixture is finely ground. Add the butter, egg, egg yolk, vanilla, and almond extract, if using. Process until well blended and smooth.

Working quickly, place each pie dough round into the pie maker. Using the accompanying pastry press, mold the dough into the wells to form the bottom crusts. (For more information on molding, see page 87.) Divide the filling among the crusts and spread evenly. Remaining almonds are used below.

Following the manufacturer's instructions, bake the pies until the crusts are well browned and the filling is puffed and slightly cracked, about 11 minutes. Using a fork, carefully lift one edge of a pie just enough to slide a small offset spatula under the bottom and transfer to a wire rack to cool slightly or completely. Repeat with the remaining pies. Serve warm or at room temperature topped with raspberries or figs, if using, a dusting of confectioners' sugar, if using, and the remaining 2 tablespoons toasted almonds.

Ginger adds a spicy fragrance to sweet plums, making them a good pairing. Plums are available in a wide array of colors: yellow, green, purple, pink, and scarlet. Any variety will be delicious in these pies.

plum-ginger pies

2 teaspoons cornstarch

2 teaspoons fresh lemon juice

2 ripe plums (about 5 oz/155 g each), rinsed and patted dry

3 tablespoons granulated sugar

1 tablespoon unsalted butter

1 teaspoon finely chopped peeled ginger

Pinch of salt

1 pie dough round for a 9- to 9½-inch (23- to 24-cm) pie (page 10)

1 frozen all-butter prepared puff pastry sheet (about 4 oz/125 g), thawed (page 10)

Vanilla ice cream for serving (optional)

makes 4 pies

To make the filling, stir together the cornstarch and lemon juice in a small bowl until dissolved. Set aside. Halve the plums, remove the pits, and cut into ½-inch (12-mm) pieces. In a frying pan over medium-low heat, cook the plums, sugar, butter, ginger, and salt, stirring until the sugar and butter are melted, about 3 minutes. Stir the cornstarch mixture and pour into the pan. Bring to a boil, continuing to stir. Boil until the plums are tender, about 1 minute. Remove from the heat. Set aside.

Following the manufacturer's instructions, preheat the electric pie maker until ready to use. Meanwhile, using the accompanying pastry cutter, cut the pie dough into 4 large rounds and cut the puff pastry into 4 small rounds. (For more information on cutting the dough, see page 87.)

Working quickly, place each large pie dough round into the pie maker. Using the accompanying pastry press, mold the dough into the wells to form the bottom crusts. (For more information on molding, see page 87.) Divide the filling among the crusts and spread evenly. Place a small puff pastry round over each filled crust.

Following the manufacturer's instructions, bake the pies until the crusts are well browned, about 10 minutes. Using a fork, carefully lift one edge of a pie just enough to slide a small offset spatula under the bottom and transfer to a wire rack to cool slightly or completely. Repeat with the remaining pies. Serve warm or at room temperature with vanilla ice cream, if using.

This classic flavor combination evokes the winter holiday season. Use ripe pears that give slightly when pressed. Buy extra cranberries to stow in the freezer and you can make these pies any time you find fresh pears.

cranberry-pear pies

1 tablespoon cornstarch

2 teaspoons fresh lemon juice

2 ripe pears (about 6 oz/185 g each), peeled and cored

2 tablespoons unsalted butter

½ cup (2 oz/60 g) fresh cranberries, rinsed and patted dry

¼ cup (2 oz/60 g) firmly packed golden brown sugar

½ teaspoon finely grated lemon zest

Pinch of salt

1 pie dough round for a 9- to 9½-inch (23- to 24-cm) pie (page 10)

1 frozen all-butter prepared puff pastry sheet (about 4 oz/125 g), thawed (page 10)

Vanilla ice cream for serving (optional)

makes 4 pies

To make the filling, stir together the cornstarch and lemon juice in a small bowl until dissolved. Set aside. Cut the pears into ½-inch (12-mm) pieces. In a frying pan over medium-low heat, melt the butter. Add the pears, cranberries, brown sugar, lemon zest, and salt. Cook, stirring, until the pears are tender and the juices are reduced, 6–8 minutes. Stir the cornstarch mixture and pour into the pan. Bring to a boil, continuing to stir. Boil until the liquid is thickened, about 1 minute. Remove from the heat and set aside.

Following the manufacturer's instructions, preheat the electric pie maker until ready to use. Meanwhile, using the accompanying pastry cutter, cut the pie dough into 4 large rounds and cut the puff pastry into 4 small rounds. (For more information on cutting the dough, see page 87.)

Working quickly, place each large pie dough round into the pie maker. Using the accompanying pastry press, mold the dough into the wells to form the bottom crusts. (For more information on molding, see page 87.) Divide the filling among the crusts and spread evenly. Place a small puff pastry round over each filled crust.

Following the manufacturer's instructions, bake the pies until the crusts are well browned, about 10 minutes. Using a fork, carefully lift one edge of a pie just enough to slide a small offset spatula under the bottom and transfer to a wire rack to cool slightly or completely. Repeat with the remaining pies. Serve warm or at room temperature with vanilla ice cream, if desired.

Cooked apples along with apple butter, cinnamon, and maple syrup are combined in these delicious little pies, bringing together the very best flavors of the fall season.

maple–apple butter pies

⅓ cup (3 oz/90 g) apple butter or pear butter

1 teaspoon cornstarch

3 tablespoons granulated sugar

2 tablespoons unsalted butter

¼ teaspoon cinnamon

Pinch of salt

1 apple (about 6 oz/185 g), peeled, cored, and cut into ¼-inch (6-mm) wedges

1 pie dough round for a 9- to 9½-inch (23- to 24-cm) pie (page 10)

⅓ cup (1½ oz/45 g) chopped pecans (optional)

4 teaspoons maple syrup

Vanilla Glaze (page 90) for garnish (optional)

makes 4 pies

To make the filling, stir together the apple butter and cornstarch in a small bowl until well blended. Set aside. In a frying pan over medium-low heat, cook the sugar, 1 tablespoon of the butter, cinnamon, and salt, stirring frequently until the sugar dissolves, about 2 minutes. Set aside and let cool. In another frying pan over medium-high heat, add the remaining 1 tablespoon butter and cook the apples, stirring, until tender, about 6 minutes. Remove from the heat and set aside to let cool.

Following the manufacturer's instructions, preheat the electric pie maker until ready to use. Meanwhile, using the accompanying pastry cutter, cut the pie dough into 4 large rounds. (For more information on cutting the dough, see page 87.)

Working quickly, place each pie dough round into the pie maker. Using the accompanying pastry press, mold the dough into the wells to form the bottom crusts. (For more information on molding, see page 87.) Divide the apple butter mixture among the crusts and spread evenly. Next, top with the cooked apples. Scatter the pecans over the top of each pie, if using.

Following the manufacturer's instructions, bake the pies until the crusts are well browned, about 10 minutes. Using a fork, carefully lift one edge of a pie just enough to slide a small offset spatula under the bottom and transfer to a wire rack to cool slightly or completely. Repeat with the remaining pies. Drizzle 1 teaspoon of the maple syrup over each pie. Serve warm or at room temperature, topped with vanilla glaze, if using.

Put your kids to work pitting the cherries for this family favorite. Pitting can be messy, so dress the kids in art smocks, set them up outside, and let them have at it. Stow extra fruit in the freezer for up to 6 months.

fresh sweet cherry pies

1 pie dough round for a 9- to 9½-inch (23- to 24-cm) pie (page 10)

1 frozen all-butter prepared puff pastry sheet (about 4 oz/125 g), thawed (page 10)

1½ cups ripe, pitted cherries (about 8 oz/250 g), rinsed and patted dry

3 tablespoons granulated sugar

2 teaspoons all-purpose flour

⅛ teaspoon pure almond extract

Pinch of salt

Vanilla ice cream for serving (optional)

makes 4 pies

Following the manufacturer's instructions, preheat the electric pie maker until ready to use. Meanwhile, using the accompanying pastry cutter, cut the pie dough into 4 large rounds and cut the puff pastry into 4 small rounds. (For more information on cutting the dough, see page 87.)

To make the filling, put the cherries in a food processor and pulse briefly until coarsely chopped. (Alternatively, chop the cherries by hand.) In a bowl, combine the chopped cherries, sugar, flour, almond extract, and salt. Stir gently to coat evenly.

Working quickly, place each large pie dough round into the pie maker. Using the accompanying pastry press, mold the dough into the wells to form the bottom crusts. (For more information on molding, see page 87.) Divide the filling among the crusts and spread evenly. Place a small puff pastry round over each filled crust.

Following the manufacturer's instructions, bake the pies until the crusts are well browned, about 10 minutes. Using a fork, carefully lift one edge of a pie just enough to slide a small offset spatula under the bottom and transfer to a wire rack to cool slightly or completely. Repeat with the remaining pies. Serve warm or at room temperature with vanilla ice cream, if desired.

Soft and sweet bananas complement salty, gooey caramel perfectly in these delicious little pies. For best results, use very ripe bananas with deep-yellow skin and lots of brown or black spots.

caramel-banana pies

1 pie dough round for a 9- to 9½-inch (23- to 24-cm) pie (page 10)

1 frozen all-butter prepared puff pastry sheet (about 4 oz/125 g), thawed (page 10)

2 very ripe bananas (about 5 oz/155 g each)

2 teaspoons all-purpose flour

Pinch of salt

¼ cup (2 fl oz/60 ml) prepared caramel sauce

Vanilla ice cream for serving (optional)

makes 4 pies

Following the manufacturer's instructions, preheat the electric pie maker until ready to use. Meanwhile, using the accompanying pastry cutter, cut the pie dough into 4 large rounds and cut the puff pastry into 4 small rounds. (For more information on cutting the dough, see page 87.)

To make the filling, peel and thinly slice the bananas. In a bowl, using a fork, combine the bananas, flour, and salt. Toss to coat evenly. Add the caramel sauce and stir with the fork, lightly smashing the bananas and coating them evenly with the sauce.

Working quickly, place each large pie dough round into the pie maker. Using the accompanying pastry press, mold the dough into the wells to form the bottom crusts. (For more information on molding, see page 87.) Divide the filling among the crusts and spread evenly. Place a small puff pastry round over each filled crust.

Following the manufacturer's instructions, bake the pies until the crusts are well browned, about 10 minutes. Using a fork, carefully lift one edge of a pie just enough to slide a small offset spatula under the bottom and transfer to a wire rack to cool slightly or completely. Repeat with the remaining pies. Serve warm or at room temperature with vanilla ice cream, if using.

Dried apricots, pears, and cherries make a flavorful filling for this recipe, but any combination of fruit would be delicious. Select plump, moist dried fruit and avoid those that look shriveled or moldy.

mixed dried fruit pies

1⅓ cups (6½ oz/200 g) diced mixed dried fruit

1 cup (8 fl oz/250 ml) apple or pear cider

3 tablespoons firmly packed golden brown sugar

½ teaspoon finely grated orange zest

½ teaspoon ground cinnamon

Pinch of salt

1 tablespoon unsalted butter

½ teaspoon pure vanilla extract

1 pie dough round for a 9- to 9½-inch (23- to 24-cm) pie (page 10)

Ice cream or Whipped Cream (page 90) for serving (optional)

makes 4 pies

To make the filling, put the dried fruit, cider, brown sugar, orange zest, cinnamon, and salt in a medium saucepan. Cook, over medium heat, stirring, until the liquid comes to a boil. Reduce the heat to low, cover, and simmer, stirring occasionally, until the fruit is tender and the liquid is reduced to a very thick, syruplike glaze, about 8 minutes. Remove from the heat. Add the butter and vanilla. Stir until the butter melts. Set aside.

Following the manufacturer's instructions, preheat the electric pie maker until ready to use. Meanwhile, using the accompanying pastry cutter, cut the pie dough into 4 large rounds. (For more information on cutting the dough, see page 87.)

Working quickly, place each pie dough round into the pie maker. Using the accompanying pastry press, mold the dough into the wells to form the bottom crusts. (For more information on molding, see page 87.) Divide the filling among the crusts and spread evenly.

Following the manufacturer's instructions, bake the pies until the crusts are well browned, about 10 minutes. Using a fork, carefully lift one edge of a pie just enough to slide a small offset spatula under the bottom and transfer to a wire rack to cool slightly. Repeat with the remaining pies. Serve warm topped with ice cream or whipped cream, if using.

These treats can be baked, cooled, and stowed in the freezer for as long as 1 month before serving. Thaw the pies and reheat them in the pie maker for 2 to 4 minutes. Brush the tops of the pies with syrup before serving.

pecan pies

1 pie dough round for a 9- to 9½-inch (23- to 24-cm) pie (page 10)

⅓ cup (3 fl oz/80 ml) golden cane syrup or light corn syrup, plus 2–3 tablespoons for brushing

⅓ cup (2½ oz/75 g) firmly packed golden or dark brown sugar

3 tablespoons unsalted butter, melted

Pinch of salt

2 large eggs

¾ teaspoon pure vanilla extract

½ cup (2 oz/60 g) chopped pecans

Vanilla ice cream or Caramel Glaze (page 90) for serving

makes 4 pies

Following the manufacturer's instructions, preheat the electric pie maker until ready to use. Meanwhile, using the accompanying pastry cutter, cut the pie dough into 4 large rounds. (For more information on cutting the dough, see page 87.)

To make the filling, combine the cane syrup, brown sugar, butter, and salt in a bowl. Whisk until smooth. Add the eggs and vanilla. Whisk until the mixture is well blended.

Working quickly, place each pie dough round into the pie maker. Using the accompanying pastry press, mold the dough into the wells to form the bottom crusts. (For more information on molding, see page 87.) Scatter the pecans evenly into each crust. Divide the filling on top of the pecans and spread evenly.

Following the manufacturer's instructions, bake the pies until the crusts are well browned, about 10 minutes. Using a fork, carefully lift one edge of a pie just enough to slide a small offset spatula under the bottom and transfer to a wire rack to cool slightly or completely. Repeat with the remaining pies. Brush the tops of the pies with the remaining syrup. Serve warm or at room temperature topped with the vanilla ice cream or glaze, if using.

For a new twist on Thanksgiving dessert, serve your guests these individual-size versions of the pie. These miniatures are easy to make any time of the year when you are nostalgic for the holiday feast.

pumpkin pies

- 1 pie dough round for a 9- to 9½-inch (23- to 24-cm) pie (page 10)
- ⅔ cup (6 oz/180 g) canned pumpkin purée
- ½ cup (3½ oz/105 g) firmly packed golden or dark brown sugar
- 2 teaspoons all-purpose flour
- 1 teaspoon ground ginger
- ¾ teaspoon ground cinnamon
- ½ teaspoon freshly grated nutmeg
- ¼ teaspoon salt
- 2 large eggs
- 1 teaspoon pure vanilla extract
- Whipped Cream (page 90) for serving

makes 4 pies

Following the manufacturer's instructions, preheat the electric pie maker until ready to use. Meanwhile, using the accompanying pastry cutter, cut the pie dough into 4 large rounds. (For more information on cutting the dough, see page 87.)

To make the filling, combine the pumpkin purée, brown sugar, flour, ginger, cinnamon, nutmeg, and salt in a bowl. Whisk until smooth. Add the eggs and vanilla. Whisk until well blended.

Working quickly, place each pie dough round into the pie maker. Using the accompanying pastry press, mold the dough into the wells to form the bottom crusts. (For more information on molding, see page 87.) Divide the filling among the crusts and spread evenly.

Following the manufacturer's instructions, bake the pies until the crusts are well browned, about 10 minutes. Using a fork, carefully lift one edge of a pie just enough to slide a small offset spatula under the bottom and transfer to a wire rack to cool slightly or completely. Repeat with the remaining pies. Serve warm or at room temperature, topped with whipped cream, if using.

These easy-to-make pies have a natural gloss worthy of any French pastry shop window. Make sure to use ripe figs that are soft with no signs of mold or bruising. The optional glaze adds another dimension of flavor.

brown sugar–fresh fig pies

1 pie dough round for a 9- to 9½-inch (23- to 24-cm) pie (page 10)

9 oz (280 g) ripe figs, rinsed and patted dry

2 teaspoons all-purpose flour

3 tablespoons firmly packed golden brown sugar

1 teaspoon pure vanilla extract

Pinch of salt

Lemon Glaze or Vanilla Glaze (page 90) for serving (optional)

makes 4 pies

Following the manufacturer's instructions, preheat the electric pie maker until ready to use. Meanwhile, using the accompanying pastry cutter, cut the pie dough into 4 large rounds. (For more information on cutting the dough, see page 87.)

To make the filling, trim the stems from the figs. If the figs are small, cut them into halves; if large, cut them into ¾-inch (2-cm) pieces. In a bowl, combine the figs, flour, brown sugar, vanilla, and salt. Stir gently to coat evenly.

Working quickly, place each pie dough round into the pie maker. Using the accompanying pastry press, mold the dough into the wells to form the bottom crusts. (For more information on molding, see page 87.) Divide the filling among the crusts and spread evenly.

Following the manufacturer's instructions, bake the pies until the crusts are well browned, about 10 minutes. Using a fork, carefully lift one edge of a pie just enough to slide a small offset spatula under the bottom and transfer to a wire rack to cool slightly or completely. Repeat with the remaining pies. Serve warm or at room temperature drizzled with lemon or vanilla glaze, if using.

Mixing apricot preserves with fresh apricots intensifies the fruit flavor and adds a subtle tang to the filling of these pies. Be sure to weigh the fruits to ensure accuracy in this recipe.

double apricot pies

- 2 teaspoons cornstarch
- 2 teaspoons fresh lemon juice
- 3 ripe apricots, about (4 oz/125 g each), halved, pitted, and cut into ½-inch (12-mm) pieces
- 2 tablespoons apricot preserves
- 2 tablespoons granulated sugar
- 1 tablespoon unsalted butter
- Pinch of salt
- ½ teaspoon pure vanilla extract
- 1 pie dough round for a 9- to 9½-inch (23- to 24-cm) pie (page 10)
- 2 frozen all-butter prepared puff pastry sheets (about 4 oz/125 g each), thawed (page 10)
- Lemon or cinnamon ice cream for serving (optional)

makes 4 pies

To make the filling, stir together the cornstarch and lemon juice in a small bowl until the cornstarch dissolves. Set aside. In a frying pan over medium-low heat, cook the apricots, preserves, sugar, butter, and salt, stirring frequently, until the sugar is melted, about 2 minutes. Stir the cornstarch mixture and pour into the pan. Bring to a boil, continuing to stir. Boil until the apricots are tender, about 1 minute. Remove from the heat. Add the vanilla. Stir gently to coat the apricots with the liquid. Set aside.

Following the manufacturer's instructions, preheat the electric pie maker until ready to use. Meanwhile, using the accompanying pastry cutter, cut the pie dough into 4 large rounds (see page 87). Following the instructions on page 88, cut and shape the puff pastry into 4 lattice tops.

Working quickly, place each large pie dough round into the pie maker. Using the accompanying pastry press, mold the dough into the wells to form the bottom crusts. (For more information on molding, see page 87.) Divide the filling among the crusts and spread evenly. Place a lattice round over each filled crust.

Following the manufacturer's instructions, bake the pies until the crusts are well browned, about 10 minutes. Using a fork, carefully lift one edge of a pie just enough to slide a small offset spatula under the bottom and transfer to a wire rack to cool slightly or completely. Repeat with the remaining pies. Serve warm or at room temperature with ice cream, if using.

Nothing puts a smile on loved ones' faces like a chocolate dessert. The addition of cream cheese to the filling gives these pies a delicious cheesecake-like flavor and texture.

chocolate cheesecake pies

1 pie dough round for a 9- to 9½-inch (23- to 24-cm) pie (page 10)

6 oz (185 g) cream cheese, at room temperature

5 tablespoons (3 oz/90 g) granulated sugar

2 oz (60 g) bittersweet chocolate, melted

1 large egg yolk

¾ teaspoon pure vanilla extract

Whipped Cream (page 90), fresh berries, or chocolate curls for garnish

makes 4 pies

Following the manufacturer's instructions, preheat the electric pie maker until ready to use. Meanwhile, using the accompanying pastry cutter, cut the pie dough into 4 large rounds. (For more information on cutting the dough, see page 87.)

To make the filling, in a bowl, combine the cream cheese and sugar. Using an electric mixer, beat until well blended and smooth. Add the melted chocolate and mix until blended. Add the egg yolk and vanilla. Beat until just blended.

Working quickly, place each pie dough round into the pie maker. Using the accompanying pastry press, mold the dough into the wells to form the bottom crusts. (For more information on molding, see page 87.) Divide the filling among the crusts and spread evenly.

Following the manufacturer's instructions, bake the pies until the crusts are well browned and the filling is puffed, about 9 minutes. Using a fork, carefully lift one edge of a pie just enough to slide a small offset spatula under the bottom and transfer to a wire rack to cool slightly or completely. Repeat with the remaining pies. Serve warm or at room temperature, topped with a dollop of whipped cream, berries, or chocolate curls.

These classic pies are fun to serve as miniatures. They are best when made with firm apples such as Cortland or Golden Delicious. Softer apples, like McIntosh, are flavorful but won't hold their shape.

classic apple pies

¼ cup (2 oz/60 g) firmly packed golden brown sugar

1½ teaspoons cornstarch

½ teaspoon cinnamon

⅛ teaspoon ground cloves

⅛ teaspoon freshly grated nutmeg

Pinch of salt

2 apples (about 6 oz/185 g each), peeled and cored

4 tablespoons (2 oz/60 g) unsalted butter

¾ teaspoon pure vanilla extract

2 pie dough rounds, each for a 9- to 9½-inch (23- to 24-cm) pie (page 10)

Cheddar cheese wedges or vanilla ice cream for serving (optional)

makes 4 pies

To make the filling, mix together the brown sugar, cornstarch, cinnamon, cloves, nutmeg, and salt in a small bowl. Set aside. Cut the apples into ½-inch (12-mm) pieces. In a frying pan over medium-low heat, melt the butter. Add the apples and cook, stirring, until tender, about 10 minutes. Add the sugar mixture, reduce the heat to low, and cook, stirring frequently, until the sugar is melted and the apples are glazed, about 2 minutes. Remove from the heat, stir in the vanilla, and set aside to cool.

Following the manufacturer's instructions, preheat the electric pie maker until ready to use. Meanwhile, using the accompanying pastry cutter, cut the pie dough into 4 large rounds and 4 small rounds. (For more information on cutting the dough, see page 87.)

Working quickly, place each large pie dough round into the pie maker. Using the accompanying pastry press, mold the dough into the wells to form the bottom crusts. (For more information on molding, see page 87.) Divide the filling among the crusts and spread evenly. Place a small pie dough round over each filled crust.

Following the manufacturer's instructions, bake the pies until the crusts are well browned, about 10 minutes. Using a fork, carefully lift one edge of a pie to slide a small offset spatula under the bottom and transfer to a wire rack to cool slightly. Repeat with the remaining pies. Serve warm with Cheddar cheese wedges or vanilla ice cream, if using.

A Latin-American treat, *dulce de leche* is made by slowly cooking sweetened milk until it caramelizes and thickens. Here, it is blended with cream cheese for a playful cross between cheesecake and pie.

dulce de leche cheesecake pies

1 pie dough round for a 9- to 9½-inch (23- to 24-cm) pie (page 10)

5 oz (155 g) cream cheese, at room temperature

½ cup (4 fl oz/125 ml) prepared *dulce de leche*, plus extra for serving

¾ teaspoon pure vanilla extract

Pinch of salt

1 large egg yolk

Chopped toasted walnuts for serving

makes 4 pies

Following the manufacturer's instructions, preheat the electric pie maker until ready to use. Meanwhile, using the accompanying pastry cutter, cut the pie dough into 4 large rounds. (For more information on cutting the dough, see page 87.)

To make the filling, in a small bowl, combine the cream cheese, *dulce de leche,* vanilla, and salt. Using an electric mixer, beat until blended and smooth. Add the egg yolk and beat until just blended.

Working quickly, place each pie dough round into the pie maker. Using the accompanying pastry press, mold the dough into the wells to form the bottom crusts. (For more information on molding, see page 87.) Divide the filling among the crusts and spread evenly.

Following the manufacturer's instructions, bake the pies until the crusts are well browned and the filling is puffed, about 9 minutes. Using a fork, carefully lift one edge of a pie just enough to slide a small offset spatula under the bottom and transfer to a wire rack to cool slightly or completely. Repeat with the remaining pies. Serve warm or at room temperature, topped with chopped walnuts and a drizzle of *dulce de leche.*

Savory Pies

This version of the classic French dish makes a quick, easy lunch when paired with a green salad. If desired, substitute cooked pancetta or bacon for the ham and any type of semi-firm cheese for the Swiss cheese.

ham and cheese mini quiches

1 pie dough round for a 9- to 9½-inch (23- to 24-cm) pie (page 10)

⅓ cup (3 fl oz/80 ml) whole milk

2 large eggs

2 teaspoons Dijon mustard

Salt and freshly ground pepper

⅔ cup (3 oz/90 g) diced cooked ham

½ cup (1½ oz/45 g) finely shredded Swiss cheese

Chopped fresh chives for garnish

makes 4 pies

Following the manufacturer's instructions, preheat the electric pie maker until ready to use. Meanwhile, using the accompanying pastry cutter, cut the pie dough into 4 large rounds. (For more information on cutting the dough, see page 87.)

To make the filling, combine the milk, eggs, and mustard. Season with salt and pepper and whisk until well blended.

Working quickly, place each pie dough round into the pie maker. Using the accompanying pastry press, mold the dough into the wells to form the bottom crusts. (For more information on molding, see page 87.) Scatter the diced ham evenly among the crusts. Pour the egg mixture evenly into each crust and top with the cheese.

Following the manufacturer's instructions, bake the pies until the filling is puffed and the crusts are well browned, about 10 minutes. Using a fork, carefully lift one edge of a pie just enough to slide a small offset spatula under the bottom and transfer to a wire rack to cool slightly. Repeat with the remaining pies. Sprinkle with the chives and serve warm.

These pies are perfect as a grab-and-go breakfast. They also can be made without cheese, cooled, and refrigerated for up to 24 hours. Reheat them for 2 or 3 minutes in the pie maker, and then top with cheese before serving.

scrambled egg and bacon pies

1 pie dough round for a 9- to 9½-inch (23- to 24-cm) pie (page 10)

4 large eggs

¼ cup (2 fl oz/60 ml) whole milk

1-2 dashes of hot-pepper sauce (optional)

Salt and freshly ground pepper

½ cup (1½ oz/45 g) diced cooked bacon

⅓ cup (1½ oz/45 g) finely shredded jalapeño jack or Cheddar cheese (optional)

makes 4 pies

Following the manufacturer's instructions, preheat the electric pie maker until ready to use. Meanwhile, using the accompanying pastry cutter, cut the pie dough into 4 large rounds. (For more information on cutting the dough, see page 87.)

To make the filling, combine the eggs, milk, hot-pepper sauce (if using), in a small bowl. Season with salt and pepper and whisk until well blended.

Working quickly, place each pie dough round into the pie maker. Using the accompanying pastry press, mold the dough into the wells to form the bottom crusts. (For more information on molding, see page 87.) Scatter the diced bacon evenly among the crusts. Divide the egg mixture evenly into each crust.

Following the manufacturer's instructions, bake the pies until the filling is puffed and the crusts are well browned, about 8 minutes. Using a fork, carefully lift one edge of a pie just enough to slide a small offset spatula under the bottom and transfer to a wire rack to cool slightly. Repeat with the remaining pies. Sprinkle the cheese, if using, evenly over the tops of the pies. Serve warm.

These south-of-the-border pies can be made with mild or hot chiles. They make an excellent side for grilled chicken. Substitute ½ cup (3 oz/90 g) diced chicken in place of the chopped chiles for a meaty variation.

green chile and cheese pies

1 pie dough round for a 9- to 9½-inch (23- to 24-cm) pie (page 10)

1 frozen all-butter prepared puff pastry sheet (about 4 oz/125 g), thawed (page 10)

2 cans (7 oz/220 g each) chopped cooked green chiles, well drained

⅔ cup shredded whole-milk mozzarella cheese

Salt and freshly ground pepper

makes 4 pies

Following the manufacturer's instructions, preheat the electric pie maker until ready to use. Meanwhile, using the accompanying pastry cutter, cut the pie dough into 4 large rounds and cut the puff pastry into 4 small rounds. (For more information on cutting the dough, see page 87.)

To make the filling, combine the chiles and cheese. Stir until well blended. (You should have about 1⅓ cups/5 oz/155 g of filling). Season with salt and pepper to taste.

Working quickly, place each large pie dough round into the pie maker. Using the accompanying pastry press, mold the dough into the wells to form the bottom crusts. (For more information on molding, see page 87.) Divide the filling among the crusts and spread evenly. Place a small puff pastry round over each filled crust.

Following the manufacturer's instructions, bake the pies until the crusts are well browned, about 10 minutes. Using a fork, carefully lift one edge of a pie just enough to slide a small offset spatula under the bottom and transfer to a wire rack to cool slightly. Repeat with the remaining pies. Serve warm.

This British favorite dates back to the Middle Ages. A combination of fruit, meat, and spices, the filling tastes best when allowed to macerate for a while but it can also be used right away.

mince pies

- 2/3 cup (3 1/4 oz/97 g) diced mixed dried fruit
- 1/2 cup (3 oz/90 g) shredded cooked pork or beef
- 1/3 cup (1 oz/30 g) shredded apple
- 1/4 cup (2 oz/60 g) firmly packed golden brown sugar
- 1/2 teaspoon finely grated lemon zest
- 1/8 teaspoon ground allspice
- Pinch of freshly grated nutmeg
- Pinch of salt
- 2 tablespoons brandy or rum
- 1 pie dough round for a 9- to 9 1/2-inch (23- to 24-cm) pie (page 10)
- 1 frozen all-butter prepared puff pastry sheet (about 4 oz/125 g), thawed (page 10)

makes 4 pies

To make the filling, combine the dried fruit, shredded pork, shredded apple, brown sugar, lemon zest, allspice, nutmeg, and salt in a bowl. Mix until well blended. Add the brandy and stir until evenly moistened. Cover and set aside, stirring frequently, for 30 minutes, or refrigerate for up to 3 weeks.

Following the manufacturer's instructions, preheat the electric pie maker until ready to use. Meanwhile, using the accompanying pastry cutter, cut the pie dough into 4 large rounds and cut the puff pastry dough into 4 small rounds. (For more information on cutting the dough, see page 87.)

Working quickly, place each large pie dough round into the pie maker. Using the accompanying pastry press, mold the dough into the wells to form the bottom crusts. (For more information on molding, see page 87.) Divide the filling among the crusts and spread evenly. Place a small puff pastry round over each filled crust.

Following the manufacturer's instructions, bake the pies until the crusts are well browned, about 10 minutes. Using a fork, carefully lift one edge of a pie just enough to slide a small offset spatula under the bottom and transfer to a wire rack to cool slightly. Repeat with the remaining pies. Serve warm.

These creative pies taste like French onion soup without the broth. Open-faced, they make a delicious first course served with a small, lightly dressed pear-walnut salad. You can also serve them as a party appetizer.

gruyère and onion pies

- 1 tablespoon unsalted butter
- 1⅓ cups (5 oz/155 g) chopped onions
- 1½ teaspoons finely chopped fresh thyme
- 2 tablespoons white wine or water, plus wine or water as needed
- 1½ teaspoons all-purpose flour
- Salt and freshly ground pepper
- 1⅓ cups (5 oz/155 g) shredded Gruyère cheese, plus ¼ cup (1 oz/30 g) shredded Gruyère cheese for serving (optional)
- 1 pie dough round for a 9- to 9½-inch (23- to 24- cm) pie (page 10)

makes 4 pies

To make the filling, in a medium frying pan over low heat, melt the butter. Add the onions and thyme and cook, stirring often, until the onions begin to brown, about 8 minutes. Add the 2 tablespoons wine and cover, reduce the heat to very low and cook, stirring often, until the onions turn a deep golden brown, 20–25 minutes. If the onions begin to stick, add additional wine, 1 tablespoon at a time. Add the flour and stir until the onions are coated. Transfer to a bowl, and season to taste with salt and pepper. Set the onions aside and let cool to room temperature, about 10 minutes.

Following the manufacturer's instructions, preheat the electric pie maker until ready to use. Meanwhile, using the accompanying pastry cutter, cut the pie dough into 4 large rounds. (For more information on cutting the dough, see page 87.)

Add the 1⅓ cups of the cheese to the onions. Working quickly, place each pie dough round into the pie maker. Using the accompanying pastry press, mold the dough into the wells to form the bottom crusts. (For more information on molding, see page 87.) Divide the onion filling among the crusts and spread evenly.

Following the manufacturer's instructions, bake the pies until the crusts are well browned, about 10 minutes. Using a fork, carefully lift one edge of a pie just enough to slide a small offset spatula under the bottom and transfer to a wire rack to cool slightly. Repeat with the remaining pies. Serve warm topped with the remaining ¼ cup (1 oz/30 g) cheese, if desired.

Perfect for hungry vegetarians, these satisfying mini pies make the most of leftover cooked vegetables. For a meaty variation, substitute cooked diced pork, chicken, ham, or beef for the zucchini.

cheesy vegetable pies

- 1 pie dough round for a 9- to 9½-inch (23- to 24-cm) pie (page 10)
- 1 frozen all-butter prepared puff pastry sheet (about 4 oz/125 g), thawed (page 10)
- ¼ cup (1 oz/30 g) lightly packed chopped cooked spinach
- ½ cup (2½ oz/75 g) diced cooked zucchini
- ⅓ cup (1½ oz/45 g) diced cooked cauliflower
- ¼ cup (1½ oz/45 g) diced cooked carrot
- ¼ cup (1½ oz/45 g) diced cooked onion
- ¼ cup (1½ oz/45 g) frozen baby peas
- 1 teaspoon chopped fresh thyme
- Salt and freshly ground pepper
- ½ cup (1½ oz/45 g) finely shredded sharp Cheddar or mozzarella cheese

makes 4 pies

Following the manufacturer's instructions, preheat the electric pie maker until ready to use. Meanwhile, using the accompanying pastry cutter, cut the pie dough into 4 large rounds and cut the puff pastry into 4 small rounds. (For more information on cutting the dough, see page 87.)

To make the filling, squeeze out any water from the spinach and add to a bowl. Break apart any clumps in the spinach. Add the zucchini, cauliflower, carrot, onion, peas, and thyme. Season to taste with salt and pepper. Stir until well mixed.

Working quickly, place each large pie dough round into the pie maker. Using the accompanying pastry press, mold the dough into the wells to form the bottom crusts. (For more information on molding, see page 87.) Divide the filling among the crusts and spread evenly. Scatter the cheese evenly over the filling. Place a small puff pastry round over each filled crust.

Following the manufacturer's instructions, bake the pies until the crusts are well browned, about 10 minutes. Using a fork, carefully lift one edge of a pie just enough to slide a small offset spatula under the bottom and transfer to a wire rack to cool slightly. Repeat with the remaining pies. Serve warm.

These creative mini pies are inspired by the ingredients used in a falafel sandwich. Here, pie dough replaces pita bread and the vegetables are piled high atop a seasoned bean filling.

middle-eastern vegetable pies

1 pie dough round for a 9- to 9½-inch (23- to 24-cm) pie (page 10)

1¼ cups (8¾ oz/ 275 g) canned small white beans, rinsed and well drained

1 tablespoon all-purpose flour

4½ teaspoons fresh lemon juice

4 teaspoons olive oil

1 teaspoon minced garlic

¾ teaspoon ground cumin

½ teaspoon ground coriander

Salt and freshly ground pepper

2 tablespoons minced green onions, plus extra for garnish

Diced tomatoes, crumbled feta, and chopped red onion for serving

makes 4 pies

Following the manufacturer's instructions, preheat the electric pie maker until ready to use. Meanwhile, using the accompanying pastry cutter, cut the pie dough into 4 large rounds. (For more information on cutting the dough, see page 87.)

To make the filling, combine the white beans, flour, lemon juice, oil, garlic, cumin, and coriander in a food processor. Season to taste with salt and pepper. Process until blended and smooth. Add the 2 tablespoons green onions and process briefly, just to mix.

Working quickly, place each pie dough round into the pie maker. Using the accompanying pastry press, mold the dough into the wells to form the bottom crusts. (For more information on molding, see page 87.) Divide the filling among the crusts and spread evenly.

Following the manufacturer's instructions, bake the pies until the crusts are well browned, about 10 minutes. Using a fork, carefully lift one edge of a pie just enough to slide a small offset spatula under the bottom and transfer to a wire rack to cool slightly. Repeat with the remaining pies. Serve warm topped with the green onions, tomatoes, feta, and red onion.

Pesto, a paste made of basil, garlic, pine nuts, Parmesan cheese, and olive oil is a delicious flavoring for chicken. Serve these savory pies along with sautéed vegetables for a perfect weeknight meal.

pesto chicken pies

1 pie dough round for a 9- to 9½-inch (23- to 24-cm) pie (page 10)

1 frozen all-butter prepared puff pastry sheet (about 4 oz/125 g), thawed (page 10)

1 cup (6 oz/185 g) diced cooked chicken

⅓ cup (2 oz/60 g) fresh, frozen, or canned corn kernels

¼ cup (2 fl oz/60 ml) prepared pesto

Salt and freshly ground pepper

⅓ cup (1½ oz/45 g) shredded whole-milk mozzarella cheese (optional)

makes 4 pies

Following the manufacturer's instructions, preheat the electric pie maker until ready to use. Meanwhile, using the accompanying pastry cutter, cut the pie dough into 4 large rounds and cut the puff pastry into 4 small rounds. (For more information on cutting the dough, see page 87.)

To make the filling, combine the chicken, corn, and pesto in a bowl. Stir until well blended. (You should have about 1⅓ cups/11 oz/330 g of filling). Season to taste with salt and pepper.

Working quickly, place each large pie dough round into the pie maker. Using the accompanying pastry press, mold the dough into the wells to form the bottom crusts. (For more information on molding, see page 87.) Divide the filling among the crusts and spread evenly. Scatter the cheese, if using, evenly over the filling. Place a small puff pastry round over each filled crust.

Following the manufacturer's instructions, bake the pies until the crusts are well browned, about 10 minutes. Using a fork, carefully lift one edge of a pie just enough to slide a small offset spatula under the bottom and transfer to a wire rack to cool slightly. Repeat with the remaining pies. Serve warm.

These family-friendly pies can be made with leftover chili instead of the filling offered here for a quick meal in less than 30 minutes. Make sure the chili isn't too liquidy—if it is, cook it down to thicken a bit before using.

chili pies

1 tablespoon olive oil

6 oz (185 g) ground beef or turkey

⅔ cup (5 oz/160 g) chunky-style tomato salsa

½ cup (3½ oz/105 g) canned black or white beans, rinsed and well drained

¾ teaspoon chili powder

Salt and freshly ground pepper

1 pie dough round for a 9- to 9½-inch (23- to 24-cm) pie (page 10)

½ cup (2 oz/60 g) shredded Cheddar or jalapeño jack cheese for serving

⅔ cup (⅔ oz/20 g) shredded iceberg lettuce for serving

makes 4 pies

To make the filling, add the oil to a frying pan and warm over medium-low heat. Add the ground beef or turkey and cook, stirring, until the meat is crumbled and cooked through, 5–7 minutes. Add the salsa, beans, and chili powder. Cook, stirring frequently, until the liquid comes to a boil. Boil, stirring frequently, until the liquid is reduced and thickened, about 2 minutes. Remove from the heat. Season to taste with salt and pepper. Set aside.

Following the manufacturer's instructions, preheat the electric pie maker until ready to use. Meanwhile, using the accompanying pastry cutter, cut the pie dough into 4 large rounds. (For more information on cutting the dough, see page 87.)

Working quickly, place each pie dough round into the pie maker. Using the accompanying pastry press, mold the dough into the wells to form the bottom crusts. (For more information on molding, see page 87.) Divide the filling among the crusts and spread evenly.

Following the manufacturer's instructions, bake the pies until the crusts are well browned, about 10 minutes. Using a fork, carefully lift one edge of a pie just enough to slide a small offset spatula under the bottom and transfer to a wire rack to cool slightly. Repeat with the remaining pies. Serve warm with cheese and lettuce sprinkled on top.

These Scandinavian-inspired pies can be made with any cooked firm-flesh fish, such as tuna or sea bass, and they are a great way to use leftovers from a previous dinner. Complete the meal with a cucumber salad.

salmon and dill pies

1 pie dough round for a 9- to 9½-inch (23- to 24-cm) pie (page 10)

1 frozen all-butter prepared puff pastry sheet (about 4 oz/125 g), thawed (page 10)

7 oz (210 g) cooked salmon, broken apart

⅓ cup (1½ oz/45 g) cooked white or brown rice

⅓ cup (1½ oz/45 g) frozen baby peas

¾ cup (2 oz/60 g) sour cream

¾ teaspoon finely chopped fresh dill or thyme

¾ teaspoon fresh lemon juice

Salt and freshly ground pepper

makes 4 pies

Following the manufacturer's instructions, preheat the electric pie maker until ready to use. Meanwhile, using the accompanying pastry cutter, cut the pie dough into 4 large rounds and cut the puff pastry into 4 small rounds. (For more information on cutting the dough, see page 87.)

To make the filling, combine the salmon, rice, peas, sour cream, dill, and lemon juice in a bowl. Stir until blended. Season to taste with salt and pepper.

Working quickly, place each large pie dough round into the pie maker. Using the accompanying pastry press, mold the dough into the wells to form the bottom crusts. (For more information on molding, see page 87.) Divide the filling among the crusts and spread evenly. Place a small puff pastry round over each filled crust.

Following the manufacturer's instructions, bake the pies until the crusts are well browned, about 10 minutes. Using a fork, carefully lift one edge of a pie just enough to slide a small offset spatula under the bottom and transfer to a wire rack to cool slightly. Repeat with the remaining pies. Serve warm.

Spices used in Middle Eastern cooking flavor these savory treats. Filo dough, a flaky alternative to pie dough, forms the top crusts and each bite is dipped into a cooling yogurt sauce to counteract the spicy lamb filling.

curried lamb pies

- 1½ teaspoons mild curry powder
- 1 teaspoon all-purpose flour
- ⅓ cup (3 fl oz/80 ml) heavy cream
- Pinch of cayenne pepper (optional)
- 1 cup (6 oz/185 g) diced cooked lamb or chicken
- ⅓ cup (1½ oz/45 g) diced cooked potatoes
- ¼ cup (1 oz/30 g) frozen baby peas
- Salt and freshly ground pepper
- 1 pie dough round for a 9- to 9½-inch (23- to 24-cm) pie (page 10)
- 3 sheets filo dough, (each a 12-by-15-inch/30-by-45-cm rectangle) thawed if frozen (page 10)
- ¼ cup (2 oz/60 g) melted butter for brushing
- Yogurt Sauce for serving (page 91)

makes 4 pies

To make the filling, put the curry powder and flour in a small frying pan and stir until blended. Add the cream. Cook, over medium-low heat, stirring until the liquid comes to a boil. Boil, stirring frequently, until the liquid is slightly reduced and thickened, about 1 minute. Stir in the cayenne pepper, if using. Remove from the heat and stir in the lamb, potatoes, and peas. Season to taste with salt and pepper. Set aside and let cool.

Following the manufacturer's instructions, preheat the electric pie maker until ready to use. Meanwhile, using the accompanying pastry cutter, cut the pie dough into 4 large rounds and set aside. Place 1 filo sheet on a flat surface and brush with a thin coating of melted butter. Stack the second sheet on top of the first and brush with butter. Repeat the process with the third filo sheet. Again, using the accompanying pastry cutter, cut the stacks of filo into 4 small rounds. (For more information on cutting, see page 87.)

Working quickly, place each large pie dough round into the pie maker. Using the accompanying pastry press, mold the dough into the wells to form the bottom crusts. (For more information on molding, see page 87.) Divide the filling among the crusts and spread evenly. Place a small filo round over each filled crust.

Following the manufacturer's instructions, bake the pies until the crusts are well browned, about 10 minutes. Using a fork, carefully lift one edge of a pie just enough to slide a small offset spatula under the bottom and transfer to a wire rack to cool slightly. Repeat with the remaining pies. Serve warm with yogurt sauce.

Perfect for brunch entertaining, you can vary the flavors of these mini quiches by substituting diced cooked ham for the bacon and shredded mozzarella cheese for the Cheddar.

bacon and potato quiches

1 pie dough round for a 9- to 9½-inch (23- to 24-cm) pie (page 10)

⅓ cup (3 fl oz/80 ml) whole milk

2 large eggs

Pinch of freshly grated nutmeg

Salt and freshly ground pepper

⅓ cup (1 oz/30 g) diced cooked bacon

⅓ cup (1¾ oz/53 g) diced cooked potato

1 tablespoon finely chopped green onion

½ cup (1½ oz/45 g) finely shredded sharp Cheddar cheese

makes 4 pies

Following the manufacturer's instructions, preheat the electric pie maker until ready to use. Meanwhile, using the accompanying pastry cutter, cut the pie dough into 4 large rounds. (For more information on cutting the dough, see page 87.)

To make the filling, combine the milk, eggs, nutmeg, and a pinch each of salt and pepper in a small bowl. Whisk until well blended.

Working quickly, place each pie dough round into the pie maker. Using the accompanying pastry press, mold the dough into the wells to form the bottom crusts. (For more information on molding, see page 87.) Scatter the bacon, potato, and green onion evenly among the crusts. Pour the egg mixture evenly into each crust.

Following the manufacturer's instructions, bake the pies until the filling is puffed and the crusts are well browned, about 8 minutes. Using a fork, carefully lift one edge of a pie just enough to slide a small offset spatula under the bottom and transfer to a wire rack to cool slightly. Repeat with the remaining pies. Sprinkle the cheese over the pies and set aside to cool slightly. Serve warm.

Pancetta is paired with mushrooms in these hearty mini pies that are perfect for a quick but filling dinner on a busy weeknight. Feel free to substitute thickly sliced, diced bacon for the pancetta.

pancetta-mushroom pies

⅓ cup (4 oz/125 g) diced pancetta

10 large button or cremini mushrooms, 10 oz (315 g) total weight, stemmed and thinly sliced

3 tablespoons diced green onions

2½ teaspoons all-purpose flour

½ teaspoon finely chopped fresh sage (optional)

Salt and freshly ground pepper

1 pie dough round for a 9- to 9½-inch (23- to 24-cm) pie (page 10)

¼ cup (1½ oz/45 g) crumbled blue cheese for garnish (optional)

makes 4 pies

To make the filling, in a frying pan over medium-low heat, cook the pancetta, stirring, until the pieces are browned and the fat is released, 4–6 minutes. Using a slotted spoon, remove the pancetta from the pan, leaving the fat behind. Increase the heat to medium. Add the mushrooms. Cook, stirring frequently, until the mushrooms are golden brown and liquid is released, 4–6 minutes. Add the reserved pancetta, green onions, flour, and sage (if using). Cook, stirring, until the mushrooms are evenly coated. Remove from the heat. Season to taste with salt and pepper. Set aside.

Following the manufacturer's instructions, preheat the electric pie maker until ready to use. Meanwhile, using the accompanying pastry cutter, cut the pie dough into 4 large rounds. (For more information on cutting the dough, see page 87.)

Working quickly, place each pie dough round into the pie maker. Using the accompanying pastry press, mold the dough into the wells to form the bottom crusts. (For more information on molding, see page 87.) Divide the filling among the crusts and spread evenly.

Following the manufacturer's instructions, bake the pies until the crusts are well browned, about 10 minutes. Using a fork, carefully lift one edge of a pie just enough to slide a small offset spatula under the bottom and transfer to a wire rack to cool slightly. Repeat with the remaining pies. Serve warm topped with cheese, if desired.

A calzone is an Italian-style pizza pocket filled with cheese, tomato sauce, and meat or vegetables. Unlike its pizza-parlor cousin, this rich, savory open-faced version uses pie dough instead of yeast-risen dough.

pepperoni "calzone" pies

1 pie dough round for a 9- to 9½-inch (23- to 24-cm) pie (page 10)

¾ cup (3 oz/90 g) diced pepperoni

¾ cup (2 oz/60 g) shredded mozzarella cheese

½ cup (4 fl oz/125 ml) prepared marinara sauce

1 tablespoon chopped fresh basil

¼ teaspoon red pepper flakes

Salt and freshly ground pepper

makes 4 pies

Following the manufacturer's instructions, preheat the electric pie maker until ready to use. Meanwhile, using the accompanying pastry cutter, cut the pie dough into 4 large rounds. (For more information on cutting the dough, see page 87.)

To make the filling, combine the pepperoni, cheese, and marinara sauce in a bowl. Mix until blended. Add the basil and red pepper flakes. Stir until blended. Season to taste with salt and pepper.

Working quickly, place each pie dough round into the pie maker. Using the accompanying pastry press, mold the dough into the wells to form the bottom crusts. (For more information on molding, see page 87.) Divide the filling among the crusts and spread evenly.

Following the manufacturer's instructions, bake the pies until the crusts are well browned and the cheese has completely melted, about 10 minutes. Using a fork, carefully lift one edge of a pie just enough to slide a small offset spatula under the bottom and transfer to a wire rack to cool slightly. Repeat with the remaining pies. Serve warm.

With their hearty vegetable and chicken filling, these savory pies are a family favorite. To save time, the filling can be made up to 2 days in advance and kept covered in the refrigerator until ready to use.

chicken potpies

- 1 tablespoon unsalted butter
- 1 tablespoon all-purpose flour
- ⅔ cup (5 fl oz/160 ml) whole milk
- 1 teaspoon Worcestershire sauce
- ⅔ cup (4 oz/125 g) diced cooked chicken
- ¼ cup (1 oz/30 g) diced cooked carrot
- ¼ cup (1 oz/30 g) diced cooked onion
- ¼ cup (1 oz/30 g) diced cooked potato
- ¼ cup (1 oz/30 g) frozen baby peas
- Salt and freshly ground pepper
- 1 pie dough round for a 9- to 9½-inch (23- to 24-cm) pie (page 10)
- 1 frozen all-butter prepared puff pastry sheet (about 4 oz/125 g), thawed (page 10)

makes 4 pies

To make the filling, in a frying pan over medium-low heat, melt the butter. Whisk in the flour and cook until light golden brown, about 2 minutes. Remove from the heat. Whisk in the milk. Place back on medium heat and bring to a boil, whisking occasionally. Boil, whisking until the mixture starts to thicken, about 2 minutes. Remove from the heat. Stir in the Worcestershire sauce.

In a bowl, combine the milk mixture, chicken, carrot, onion, potato, and peas. Stir until well blended. Season to taste with salt and pepper. Set aside.

Following the manufacturer's instructions, preheat the electric pie maker until ready to use. Meanwhile, using the accompanying pastry cutter, cut the pie dough into 4 large rounds and cut the puff pastry into 4 small rounds. (For more information on cutting the dough, see page 87.)

Working quickly, place each large pie dough round into the pie maker. Using the accompanying pastry press, mold the dough into the wells to form the bottom crusts. (For more information on molding, see page 87.) Divide the filling among the crusts and spread evenly. Place a small puff pastry round over each filled crust.

Following the manufacturer's instructions, bake the pies until the crusts are browned, about 10 minutes. Using a fork, carefully lift one edge of a pie just enough to slide a small offset spatula under the bottom and transfer to a wire rack to cool slightly. Repeat with the remaining pies. Serve warm.

Most likely created for Cornwall tin miners, pasties are a longtime lunch favorite all over Great Britain and Ireland. Made with beef and vegetables, these little treats will keep you satisfied until dinnertime.

cornish pasties

1 tablespoon unsalted butter

1 tablespoon all-purpose flour

⅔ cup (5 fl oz/160 ml) beef broth

1 teaspoon Worcestershire sauce

½ cup (3 oz/90 g) diced cooked steak or roast beef

¼ cup (1 oz/30 g) frozen baby peas

¼ cup (1 oz/30 g) diced cooked carrot

¼ cup (1 oz/30 g) diced cooked onion

¼ cup (1 oz/30 g) diced cooked turnip or sweet potato

Salt and freshly ground pepper

1 pie dough round for a 9- to 9½-inch (23- to 24-cm) pie (page 10)

1 frozen all-butter prepared puff pastry sheet (about 4 oz/125 g), thawed (page 10)

makes 4 pies

To make the filling, in a small frying pan over medium-low heat, melt the butter. Whisk in the flour and cook until golden brown, about 3 minutes. Remove from the heat. Whisk in the broth. Return to medium heat and bring to a boil, whisking occasionally. Boil, whisking until slightly thickened, about 2 minutes. Remove from the heat. Stir in the Worcestershire sauce.

In a large bowl, combine the broth mixture, steak, peas, carrot, onion, and turnip. Stir until well blended. (You should have about 1⅓ cups/5 oz/155 g). Season with salt and pepper. Set aside.

Following the manufacturer's instructions, preheat the electric pie maker until ready to use. Meanwhile, using the accompanying pastry cutter, cut the pie dough into 4 large rounds and cut the puff pastry into 4 small rounds. (For more information on cutting the dough, see page 87.)

Working quickly, place each large pie dough round into the pie maker. Using the accompanying pastry press, mold the dough into the wells to form the bottom crusts. (For more information on molding, see page 87.) Divide the filling among the crusts and spread evenly. Place a small puff pastry round over each filled crust.

Following the manufacturer's instructions, bake the pies until the crusts are well browned, about 10 minutes. Using a fork, lift one edge of a pie just enough to slide a small offset spatula under the bottom and transfer to a wire rack to cool slightly. Repeat with the remaining pies. Serve warm.

Shepherd's pie is traditionally made with lamb, here it is made with beef or turkey and is mixed with gravy and vegetables and then topped with mashed potatoes. Variations of this classic can be found all over the world.

shepherd's pies

- 1 tablespoon olive oil
- 6 oz (185 g) ground beef or turkey
- ⅓ cup (2 oz/60 g) diced cooked onion
- ¼ cup (1½ oz/45 g) diced cooked carrot
- 1 tablespoon all-purpose flour
- ½ cup (4 fl oz/125 ml) beef broth
- 1 tablespoon Worcestershire sauce
- ½ teaspoon chopped fresh thyme
- ¼ cup (1½ oz/45 g) frozen baby peas
- Salt and freshly ground pepper
- 1 pie dough round for a 9- to 9½-inch (23- to 24-cm) pie (page 10)
- 1¼ cups (11 oz/330 g) hot cooked mashed potatoes
- 2 tablespoons chopped fresh parsley for garnish

makes 4 pies

To make the filling, in a frying pan over medium low heat, warm the oil. Add the beef, onion, and carrot. Cook, stirring, until the meat is cooked through, 5–7 minutes. Add the flour. Cook, stirring, until the flour is golden brown, about 30 seconds. Add the broth, Worcestershire sauce, and thyme. Raise the heat to medium and cook, scraping up any brown bits from the pan bottom, until the liquid comes to a boil. Boil, stirring, until the liquid is reduced, about 2 minutes. Remove from the heat. Stir in the peas. Season to taste with salt and pepper. Set aside.

Following the manufacturer's instructions, preheat the electric pie maker until ready to use. Meanwhile, cut the pie dough into 4 large rounds. (For more information on cutting the dough, see page 87.)

Working quickly, place each pie dough round into the pie maker. Using the accompanying pastry press, mold the dough into the wells to form the bottom crusts. (For more information on molding, see page 87.) Divide the filling among the crusts and spread evenly.

Following the manufacturer's instructions, bake the pies until the crusts are well browned and the filling is heated through, about 10 minutes. Using a fork, carefully lift one edge of a pie just enough to slide a small offset spatula under the bottom and transfer to a wire rack to cool slightly. Repeat with the remaining pies. Serve warm topped with mashed potatoes and a sprinkle of parsley.

These Greek-inspired pies make a perfect light supper when paired with a Greek salad of cucumbers, tomatoes, and olives. For a meaty version, substitute ⅓ cup (2½ oz/75 g) of diced, cooked ham for some of the spinach.

spinach and feta pies

1 pie dough round for a 9- to 9½-inch (23- to 24-cm) pie (page 10)

10 oz (315 g) frozen chopped spinach, thawed and squeezed dry

5 tablespoons (3 fl oz/80 ml) heavy cream

3 tablespoons finely chopped green onions

2–4 drops of hot-pepper sauce

Salt and freshly ground pepper

⅔ cup (3½ oz/105 g) crumbled feta cheese

makes 4 pies

Following the manufacturer's instructions, preheat the electric pie maker until ready to use. Meanwhile, using the accompanying pastry cutter, cut the pie dough into 4 large rounds. (For more information on cutting the dough, see page 87.)

To make the filling, squeeze out any water from the spinach and add to a large bowl. Break apart any clumps in the spinach. Add the cream, green onions, hot-pepper sauce, and salt and pepper to taste. Mix until well blended. Add half of the cheese and mix again just until blended.

Working quickly, place each pie dough round into the pie maker. Using the accompanying pastry press, mold the dough into the wells to form the bottom crusts. (For more information on molding, see page 87.) Divide the filling among the crusts and spread evenly. Scatter the remaining cheese evenly over the filling.

Following the manufacturer's instructions, bake the pies until the crusts are well browned, about 10 minutes. Using a fork, carefully lift one edge of a pie just enough to slide a small offset spatula under the bottom and transfer to a wire rack to cool slightly. Repeat with the remaining pies. Serve warm.

Spicy chorizo combined with salty Spanish-style manchego cheese, peppers, and olives turn these mini pies into a variation on pizza. If manchego is unavailable, mozzarella can be used in its place.

chorizo, pepper, and olive pies

1 pie dough round for a 9- to 9½-inch (23- to 24-cm) pie (page 10)

⅔ cup (4 oz/120 g) diced fully cooked, Spanish-style chorizo

⅓ cup (1½ oz/75 g) shredded manchego cheese

¼ cup (2 oz/60 g) chopped cooked or roasted red bell pepper

¼ cup (1½ oz/75 g) chopped pitted Spanish olives

Salt and freshly ground pepper

makes 4 pies

Following the manufacturer's instructions, preheat the electric pie maker until ready to use. Meanwhile, using the accompanying pastry cutter, cut the pie dough into 4 large rounds. (For more information on cutting the dough, see page 87.)

To make the filling, in a bowl, combine the chorizo, cheese, bell pepper, and olives. Stir until well blended. (You should have about 1⅓ cups/11 oz/330 g of filling.) Season to taste with salt and pepper.

Working quickly, place each pie dough round into the pie maker. Using the accompanying pastry press, mold the dough into the wells to form the bottom crusts. (For more information on molding, see page 87.) Divide the filling among the crusts and spread evenly.

Following the manufacturer's instructions, bake the pies until the crusts are well browned and the filling is heated through, about 10 minutes. Using a fork, lift one edge of a pie just enough to slide a small offset spatula under the bottom and transfer to a wire rack to cool slightly. Repeat with the remaining pies. Serve warm.

These open-faced pies are reminiscent of twice-baked potatoes with bits of steak mixed in. The best part is that you can use the leftovers from a steak-and-potatoes dinner for a quick meal. Serve with a green salad.

steak and potato pies

1 pie dough round for a 9- to 9½-inch (23- to 24-cm) pie (page 10)

1 cup (9 oz/280 g) cooked mashed potatoes

⅔ cup (4 oz/125 g) diced cooked steak, chicken, or ham

¼ cup (1 oz/30 g) shredded Cheddar cheese, plus ¼ cup (1 oz/30 g) shredded Cheddar cheese for garnish (optional)

3 tablespoons chopped green onions

Salt and freshly ground pepper

makes 4 pies

Following the manufacturer's instructions, preheat the electric pie maker until ready to use. Meanwhile, using the accompanying pastry cutter, cut the pie dough into 4 large rounds. (For more information on cutting the dough, see page 87.)

To make the filling, in a bowl, combine the mashed potatoes, steak, ¼ cup (1 oz/30 g) of the cheese, and green onions. Stir until well blended. (You should have about 1⅓ cups/11 oz/330 g of filling.) Season to taste with salt and pepper.

Working quickly, place each pie dough round into the pie maker. Using the accompanying pastry press, mold the dough into the wells to form the bottom crusts. (For more information on molding, see page 87.) Divide the filling among the crusts and spread evenly.

Following the manufacturer's instructions, bake the pies until the crusts are well browned and the filling is heated through, about 10 minutes. Using a fork, carefully lift one edge of a pie just enough to slide a small offset spatula under the bottom and transfer to a wire rack to cool slightly. Sprinkle with the remaining ¼ cup cheese, if using. Repeat with the remaining pies. Serve warm.

basic techniques

working with the dough

The electric pie maker comes equipped with a customized pastry cutter to cut out dough rounds for each mini pie, as well as a special pastry press to mold the dough into shape once it has been placed in the pie maker.

1 roll out the dough (optional)

If you've purchased pie dough, it might need to be rolled out slightly to accommodate four large dough rounds. While the pie maker preheats, lightly flour a work surface and a rolling pin. Place the dough onto the work surface and lightly dust the top with flour. Rolling from the center toward the edges and in all directions, roll out the dough until it is ⅛ inch (3 mm) thick or until 4 large rounds can be cut from it. Work quickly to prevent the dough from becoming warm. If the dough sticks to the work surface, add more flour and loosen it with a flat tool such as a bench scraper or an offset spatula.

2 cut out the rounds

Place the large side of the pastry cutter included with the electric pie maker near an edge of the dough round and press down firmly. Avoid twisting the cutter because it can tear the dough. Repeat 3 times until you have 4 rounds. Some recipes also call for top crusts—in that case, cut 4 top crusts with the small side of the pastry cutter. (If using filo dough, turn to page 10 for instructions.)

3 mold the crust

When the pie maker has finished preheating and the ready light comes on, open the lid and, working quickly, gently fit a dough round over the center of each pie well. Place the pastry press over the dough in the well and gently push down until the dough just covers the mold's crimped edge.

4 seal the pies (optional)

After adding the filling, if you are making a pie with a top crust, place a small dough round on top of the filled crust. When you close the machine's lid, the top and bottom crusts will be sealed closed and it will form a decorative crimped edge.

dough cutouts

If you have extra dough, cut shapes to decorate the top crusts of the pies. Before baking, press the dough scraps together. On a floured work surface and using a floured rolling pin, roll out the dough until it is ⅛ inch (3 mm) thick. Using a small cookie cutter, cut out shapes. Using a flat spatula, lift the shapes and place on the top crust of your pie. Bake according to the manufacturer's instructions.

making a lattice top

A lattice top looks extra special on a mini pie. For pies made in an electric pie maker, the traditional technique changes slightly and light and flaky puff pastry dough (see page 10) works best. You'll need 2 prepared puff pastry sheets.

1 cut the lattice strips

Lay 2 sheets of thawed puff pastry on a lightly floured work surface. Using a sharp knife or pastry wheel, cut one puff pastry sheet into 4 vertical strips, each about ¾ inch (2 cm) wide.

2 create the lattice pattern

Beginning at about the center of the puff pastry sheet, set two strips vertically on top of the pastry sheet, spacing them about 1 inch (2.5 cm) apart. Next, fold back the vertical strip closest to the left and place a horizontal strip beneath it. Fold the strip back down and then place the rest of the horizontal strip over the top part of the next vertical strip. Repeat with a second horizontal strip but reverse the direction (see photo). Repeat the process to cover the entire sheet with lattice strips using the remaining strips.

3 cut the lattice top

Place the smaller side of the pastry cutter over the top of the lattice pattern and puff pastry sheet and cut out one small round of dough. Cut out the remaining lattice tops and set aside.

4 transfer the lattice top

Using a wide flat spatula, carefully transfer the lattice-covered dough cutout to the top of a filled crust in the preheated electric pie maker. Working quickly, repeat steps 3 and 4 to cover the remaining filled crusts. Follow the manufacturer's instructions to bake the pies.

dough tips & tricks

Working with dough can be challenging. Here are a few tips to help you along.

- Puff pastry dough can be sticky. To make it easier to roll, place it between two sheets of wax paper.
- Sprinkling a little flour over the dough will make molding a crust in the electric pie maker easier.
- To get smooth edges on your pie bases and tops, press straight down with the pastry cutter.
- Dough can be precut ahead of time, wrapped in plastic wrap, and stored in the freezer.
- Use frozen dough as soon as it has thawed. If it sits out too long, it will be difficult to work with.

basic recipes

chocolate glaze

½ cup (4 fl oz/125 ml) heavy cream

4 tablespoons (2 oz/60 g) unsalted butter, cut into ½-inch (12-mm) cubes

3 tablespoons light corn syrup

4 oz (125 g) semisweet chocolate, finely chopped

1 teaspoon pure vanilla extract

In a saucepan over medium heat, combine the cream, butter, and corn syrup and cook, stirring, until the butter melts and the mixture is hot but not boiling. Remove from the heat and add the chocolate. Let stand for 30 seconds, then stir until the chocolate is completely melted and the glaze is smooth. Stir in the vanilla. Let cool until thickened, about 20 minutes.

makes about 1 cup (8 fl oz/250 ml)

caramel glaze

2 tablespoons unsalted butter

¼ cup (2 oz/60 g) firmly packed dark brown sugar

1 tablespoon heavy cream

½ cup (2 oz/60 g) confectioners' sugar

In a saucepan over medium heat, combine the butter, brown sugar, and cream. Cook, stirring, until the mixture is hot but not boiling. Remove from the heat and let cool slightly, about 1 minute. Stir in the confectioners' sugar until well blended. Let cool until thickened, about 20 minutes.

makes about 1 cup (8 fl oz/250 ml)

vanilla glaze

2 cups (8 oz/250 g) confectioners' sugar

¼ cup (2 fl oz/60 ml) plus 2 tablespoons heavy cream

1 teaspoon pure vanilla extract

In a large bowl, sift the confectioners' sugar. Add the cream and vanilla and stir until the glaze is smooth, about 1 minute.

makes about 1 cup (8 fl oz/250 ml)

lemon glaze

2 cups confectioners' (8 oz/250 g) sugar

¼ cup (2 fl oz/60 ml) plus 2 tablespoons heavy cream

1 teaspoon fresh lemon juice

In a large bowl, sift the confectioners' sugar. Add the cream and lemon juice and stir until the glaze is smooth, about 1 minute.

makes about 1 cup (8 fl oz/250 g)

whipped cream

1 cup (8 fl oz/250 ml) heavy cream

1 tablespoon granulated sugar

1 teaspoon pure vanilla extract

In a large bowl, combine the cream, sugar, and vanilla. Using an electric mixer set on medium-high speed, beat until soft, billowy peaks form, about 2 minutes. Cover the bowl and refrigerate for up to 2 hours.

makes about 2 cups (16 fl oz/500 ml)

yogurt sauce

1 cup (8 oz/250 g) plain whole-milk yogurt

1 small clove garlic, minced

1½ tablespoons fresh lemon juice

2 tablespoons chopped fresh mint

¼ teaspoon sea salt

In a small bowl, stir together the yogurt, garlic, lemon juice, mint, and salt until well blended.

makes about 1 cup (8 fl oz/250 ml)

basic pie dough

1¼ cups (6¼ oz/200 g) all-purpose flour

1 tablespoon granulated sugar

¼ teaspoon salt

¼ cup (4 oz/125 g) cold unsalted butter, cut into ½-inch (12-mm) cubes

3 tablespoons cold trans fat-free vegetable shortening, cut into ¾-inch (2-cm) pieces

3 tablespoons very cold water

To make the dough in a food processor, fit the processor with a metal blade. Add the flour, sugar, and salt to the processor's work bowl and pulse to blend. Add the pieces of butter and shortening and pulse until the texture resembles coarse cornmeal, with the butter and shortening reduced to ½-inch (12-mm) pieces. Add the water a little at a time and pulse just until the dough just begins to come together in a rough mass.

To make the dough by hand, combine the flour, sugar, and salt in a large bowl. Add the pieces of butter and shortening and toss to coat with flour. Using a pastry blender or 2 knives, cut the pieces of butter and shortening into the flour mixture and toss with a fork until the dough until the texture resembles coarse cornmeal, with the butter and shortening reduced to ½-inch (12-mm) pieces. Add the water a little at a time and pulse just until the dough just begins to come together in a rough mass.

Remove the dough to a work surface and shape into a 5-inch (13-cm) disk. Wrap in plastic and refrigerate until well chilled, at least 2 hours.

makes one 9- to 9½-inch (23- to 24-cm) dough round

index

weldon**owen**

415 Jackson Street, Suite 200, San Francisco, CA 94111
Telephone: 415 291 0100 Fax: 415 291 8841
www.wopublishing.com

Weldon Owen is a division of
BONNIER

WELDON OWEN, INC.

CEO and President Terry Newell
VP, Sales and Marketing Amy Kaneko
Director of Finance Mark Perrigo

VP and Publisher Hannah Rahill
Executive Editor Jennifer Newens
Editor Donita Boles

Creative Director Emma Boys
Art Director Alexandra Zeigler
Designer Rachel Lopez Metzger

Production Director Chris Hemesath
Production Manager Michelle Duggan
Color Manager Teri Bell

Photographer Lauren Burke
Food Stylist Robyn Valarik
Prop Stylist Ethel Brennan

MINI PIES

Conceived and produced by Weldon Owen, Inc.

Color separations by Embassy Graphics in Canada
Printed and bound by 1010 Printing, Ltd. in China

First printed in 2011
10 9 8

Library of Congress Control Number:
2010941206

ISBN-13: 978-1-61628-123-6
ISBN-10: 1-61628-123-5

ACKNOWLEDGMENTS

Weldon Owen wishes to thank the following people for their generous support in producing this book:
Linda Bouchard, Kimberly Chun, Ken DellaPenta, Sean Franzen, Stacey Glick, Alexa Hyman, Lauren Ladoceour, and Lesli Neilson.